New Uses for a Wand

Fiona Theokritoff

Five Leaves Publications

New Uses for a Wand
Fiona Theokritoff

Published in 2024 by Five Leaves Publications
14a Long Row, Nottingham NG1 2DH
www.fiveleaves.co.uk
www.fiveleavesbookshop. co.uk

ISBN: 978-1-915434-16-6

Printed in Great Britain

Contents

For my very own team GB, with love

Eutectic

Welcome to my cupboard of imperfect treasures:

a muttering of wood ash develops
alchemical blush of barium, titanium –
everything brought to light.

Malleable as clay, I unwrap myself
offer you my wares, my stories'
glinting wit of iridescence.

The cracks and dunts are part of this too,
twice-fired by life, and scared by it all,
brittle as biscuit.

Still, despite and because,
I will step into the kiln with you.
Discover where the hottest places are.

Hag Stone

A stone with a hole in it,
scoured, round and perfect.
The stone is. The hole is.
There was no plan,
simply grains grinding on stone,
smaller stone on bigger stone.
I put my eye to the hole.

Through the hole we saw
what we wanted to see,
filled the hole with stories
of snakes, charms, enchanted lands.
The hole was filled with eons, epochs, eras,
more time than we could imagine.
It was easier to believe in stories.

Lazulum

Perhaps, long ago, the sky fell in and trapped
pieces of heaven in these sun-scorched rocks.
With time they revealed a blue miracle.

sun in the sky
yellow in the blue

Egyptian amulet with a scarab in blue lapis:
the humble toiling beetle. A life of rolling,
as the sun's barge rolls across the sky.

sun spans the sky
yellow in the blue

Powdered blue combines with oils and waxes
into a benediction of colour. Scribes bring
heaven's promise to expectant vellum.

halo in the sky
yellow in the blue

More precious than gold, this ultramarine
cloaks Titian's Madonnas, adorns
the subjects of Vermeer's obsession.

stone of the sky
yellow in the blue

Volcanic heat petrified blue sky, locked in
brimstone. Rock of changes: the fabled, the fabulous,
the yellow in the blue.

sulphur in the stone
yellow in the blue

Cwen

My king is dead.
I held him many times blood-slicked
and battle-dazed, in defeat or victory.
My bedmate and eager lover is gone.
I am no longer Raedwald's Cwen,
but Cwen I am still. I command the house.
My chatelaine has keys to all the coffers,
my power is visible, like his.

Listen as I sing of him, your keeper, your king,
loved by the battle-brothers he gathered
round him in his haven-hall. He blessed you
with mead and treasure: you gave everything for him.

He listened to my counsel. I nudged him back
to our heart-held ways, ancient ties
of guest-greeting, bonds of kinship.
Cwen I am here, bound to men of blood and action,
braided with the blood-threads of peace pledge.
I trust in threads spun from true talk, fine yet strong.
Fast in the weave, lissom in their movement,
and brilliant with the colours of happy goodwill.

Cwen I am here. My weaving women sing
with the skills in their fingers: I will have the finest cloth
for his clothes, tablet-woven madder red and weld yellow.
Combined, deft as his pattern-welded sword.

His strong body lies stilled. It will leave washed,
free of the stink and stench of battle, shaved,
smelling skin-sweet. He needs his beard-oils with him,
his weapons bright with garnets, his lyre,
his feasting pots to welcome fighting friends.

His most trusted brothers will shoulder the ship,
treasured king inside, into the riverway deeps,
and he will make swift passage to the death-hall
beyond our world of water and land, earth and sky.

Your Cwen commands it.

Smickling

I am as useless as a coronet,
have lost a shoal of bloodied runts.
Who shall assist me?

Perhaps a ripe and red-faced
peasant with more brats
than she can raise.

I need her shoes,
I need a charm to stick
what quickens to its cage.

Perhaps the retching servant girl,
put away once her belly swelled.
Or you: with a brood already, lioness.

Your shoes, near my own in size and elegance –
not brutal things for labouring –
caress your white feet, so dainty.

Wearing them, I will know your shape,
that noble arch, feel the pink shells
of your toenails' impressions.

I need just one mewling infant
to stride a man, to rule this jostle
of land and trade. Just one.

Pilgrim

To the
home of wise
Ælred I come for salve
and salvation. Look on my feet,
these ulcerous slabs, and pity me. I
offer a shoe in soft lead. A lay-brother,
I tipped up the crucible roughly, mistook
myself the butt of young Brother Thomas'
teasing. My blunder burned him, my own
feet too, blistered in the molten spread.
He is whole once more, but my ulcers
gnaw deeper with heat of my anger
unforgiven. A simple man, no
citizen of the metaphysical
world, I beg a simple
forgiveness. And a
simple Earth physic
to help me too; the
plant that shrieks
echoes my mewling
as my stained bindings
are unwound. With the
blessing of healed flesh
I shall walk with a new
purpose, transfigured
from my base
lead life.

The World Turns

She places on her cool wrist
a bracelet which contains time.
On this clock face, the hours
are fragments of our human story.
The tick of iridescent glass,
the tock of sweet-shop smalti,
shells dredged from the world's shores,
Aunt Sadie's pearls, walk-worn tiles,
silver coins and battle medals.
Willow pattern's distant chatter,
clay pipes filled with long-stilled breath.

Her eyes see, as eyes have always seen,
the world that turns
earth and fire, air and water,
wood and metal into mud.
Time compressed into sediments at rest.
Until, unearthed by mudlark's curiosity,
her spark of alchemy transforms
base metal of experience
into this object of gold.
And the world turns again.

AKA Janus

Isaac stands in his Cambridge doorway
back-lit by familiar bonfires of old magic,
the rosy-gold glow of alchemy.
He peers forward into a clear white future,
burns to enlighten the world, find
new uses for a wand.

As London convulses with plague, pox and flame,
this country lad works in scholars' grounds.
His focused thoughts illuminate science
up ahead, submit light to prisms: see it split,
visible in seven colours, then recombined
to transparency with another.

Interesting times. He pins his colours
to the new world flag, obfuscates his love affair
with the old ways. More than two centuries pass.
After mud, blood and trench, his seven colours
are co-opted by another Englishman, painting
Eastern energy for Western minds.

Ancient and new-age mystics gather under
the over-arching chakra rainbow. Newton's universe.
As above, so below.

Photosynthesis

Magnesium – Mg2+ – activates enzymes in phosphate metabolism.
Constituent of chlorophyll.
Biology: A Functional Approach, MBV Roberts

The Magus takes centre stage,
and in his own limelight,
creates alchemy
with simple wandering players:

$$6CO_2 + 6H_2O \xrightarrow{\text{sunlight}} C_6H_{12}O_6 + 6O_2$$

Photons cascade through stacks
of green lamellae coins, exchange
one currency for another.

Sugar strings will become
coiled sugar rings,
a chorus line of can-can dancers,
energy locked in their sweet skirts.

Released, that sun-sparked flash
means a flower will bloom,
a grub will feed.

Green blood throbs.
Silent Magus sits.

Ballet Shoe Factory

A grimy fairyland where
many times upon a last, shoes appear.

He who owns the crown is the king of makers,
his domain a pot of secret paste, a bench

where – mere subject now – he layers paper, burlap,
canvas, satin. Each day, he turns the ugly duckling shoes

right side out over a witch's broomstick.
As satin swans, he pushes them

into an oven big enough for Hansel and Gretel.
Overnight, they bake: soft satin with an iron-hard block.

Finished with silky ribbons to bind a maker's skills
with fierce muscles, fine bones,

that will endure the crush of overstrain
for long hours, days, years.

Brave New World

I

We survive one war and hold our breath
for another.

Dressed like a deco cinema, the wooden cabinet
was made in green St Albans.

In a world suddenly grown smaller, watching
is everything. Your children's toes

are exposed to its X-ray inspection,
and kept glowing straight.

Step into shoe-shaped slots,
and we will peer at your feet

through our triple viewers, our
Pedoscope machines. Thirty years

since Roentgen's super vision,
see-through sight is on every High Street.

II

New Jersey girls purse their mouths
to a fine point: 'lip, dip and paint, girls'.

Safe in this science age, Undark paint
lights dials in military darkness.

In the dimmed washroom, the girls giggle over
glowing teeth and wandering green fingernails.

Feeling breathless? That's from dancing late.
And those problems with your jaw?

Our lawyers say it's syphilis: be careful
of the company you keep, girls.

From Morayshire to Gloucestershire, those dials burn
as post-war scrap. Radium contaminates the soil.

Years later, the green light comes for new homes.

Shoes on the Danube

Sixty pairs of cast-iron shoes,
one pair for each year since 1945
when thousands stepped out from theirs, stripped,
and were shot into cold December waters.

Stand in those shoes.

A shriek away from Parliament,
the worn-out dichotomies of us and them,
welcome and not, citizen and alien,
still raise fences, build railways to dead-end destinations.

Strike Hard, Strike Sure

4000lb bomb hoist point cover, starting handle
       engine combustion chamber
              main fuel cock, jacking point

turn buckle, oxygen pipe run in
       navigator's protractor
              centre of artificial horizon

rudder hinge, quick release pin
       base of flare cartridge
              slow running cut out, exhaust pipes

pip squeak panel, bomb shackle
       searchlight fuse, air speed indicator face,
              flying helmet earphone

landing light switch, signal flare tins
       0.5 inch shells, pressure gauge
              .303 inch bullets

end of control rod, altimeter gauge face
       wing, corrugated inner skin
              wireless valve, hinge from Elsan toilet lid

auto-pilot remains
       battery terminal end
              non-return valve.

No Dolls

It had been pink once, pink and soft and fluffy, cut down from a blanket, but the twiddling action of small finger and thumb had worn the fluff away, exposed a skeleton of fibres in bare patches. It tucked in as I turned over to sleep, hunkered down near my shoulder where I could feel its still-softness on my cheek, smell its biscuity animal warmth. It was terrible when Mum washed it. Lost, the safe warm smell of my hot hands smeared on my comfy. I had to twiddle and knead it all over again, until it was safe to go on the dark path.

Estuarine

I grew where the flat brown earth
speaks of borrowing, not taking,
of exchange, not change.

I learned to read
my mother's compressed lips. Her words
spent as carefully as coins.

But I yearned for extravagance,
sought out dramatic word topography:
the impossible, fantastic, phantasmagoric.

I braved steep inclines of rising intonation,
the sheer drop of an exclamation mark.
I even tackled wild cliffs of exaggeration.

Now instead, I merge with silky silty mud, clinging
moisture-heavy round my legs,
dried to a second skin I thought I'd shed.

Soil and seed have long memories.
They wait until they germinate
in my mouth, the mouth my mother gave me.

My Mother Left Me Her Store of Blackberry Vinegar

We gathered them in colanders, boxes,
skirt-buckets, each plump berry ripe
from a summer's worth of sun.

We spread our black treasures
in dishes, left them to steep
in the drip and tang of vinegar.

Muslin-strained for twelve hours,
finger-stained with love.

Boil fast, sugar rush then
bottle and cool, store and wait.

Wait until sweetened beyond acid.
This may take years.

Husks

Wartime childhoods allowed no waste.
So Mum and Dad's shoes
are never thrown away.

They slide slow and undignified from best
to everyday
to garden.

Two pairs lean into each other
on muddied newspaper,
wrinkled, but soldiering on.

Hers are black, once-shiny buckles
tarnished and grimed,
ground down at the heel.

His clean brown lace-ups
sit empty like seed husks,
too fragile to burden with tasks.

But –
one of these days.
When he's up to it.

Charm

How much luck do you need?
You're the ones with the big house
and clean hands.
What use are hobnails with
their heads worn down –
rotting laces overstretched by the pull
of early starts?

The new-laid rich brown boards stretch away,
their straight lines crisper than the loamy furrows
that my brothers and your horses plough.
We all labour quietly, those beneath us
who mine the blackness, the grubbiest of all.
Our bird-light bodies dusty inside and out:
ragged breath, ragged trousers.
We groom your vistas, charm your lives.

Your soft calf slippers waltz across the oak.

Dance Number

Mendeleev spread it before us – his table of the elements,
another map of our world. On posters it's multicoloured:
an illuminated dance floor for atomic numbers,
shuffled into a line-dance of groups and rows.

Element 1, Hydrogen. Top left, it is gaseous and flirty:
an electron to spare, ready to pair up
with any partner, dance the electron boogie.
Choreograph the chemistry of water.

Element 2, Helium. Right against the wall, with those
whose dance-card electron shells are already filled.
Nothing to share except a noble sangfroid:
never react, never respond, never explain. Just glow.

The rest cha-cha-cha from left to right,
from volatility to stability. Weighed down
by increasing mass and number, they must be
jostled, irritated or heated to pair up,

won't tango with just any element,
but find a dance partner with a matching spark.

Hymn to a Mycelium

Behold   the hidden

                       the beneath
            the underground.

This creeping life weaves
                connections
        between roots
           and rocks.

A scavenger shows no
                judgement: with death
                                there's growth.

Hyphae threads grow a sunless city that   never sleeps
           beats with the rhythm of mycelium.

Perceiving alien
     throbs invisible
          a trip beyond gravity
             beyond logic

        shares itself with forest shrubs
        pierces their roots
        exchanges elements
        links ash
           to oak
               to beech
                  to birch
        in humble silence

        propagates problem-solving networks
           that the human animal has only now devised.

Our craniums
birth our systems whole   your systems
                 grow   cell
                           by cell
                           by cell.
                                      left or right?
                                      left or right?
                                      blind watchmaker
                                      tick or tock?

We have no citizen body like yours,
but
             your visions boost our lives,
                         your brews blur our senses,
                    dissolve our oneness
                              into unity.

Just for a while.

Opportunity's Knock

When an unstoppable asteroid met
an immovable Earth
Most winged lives stopped, then dropped.
Dinosaurs vaporised in an instant,
ground-dwellers dead in their tracks:
only carrion-eaters left.

The ocean became an acid bath, liquefied
all but persistent reptilians, crocodilians.
The end of an era cast a geologic trace:
a space-gifted iridium layer,
the asteroid's line in the sand.

We mammals adapted fast: moved in,
moved up, settled our proto-arses into
spare niches, got clever, captured time.
Calculated distances, trajectories and orbits
live on-screen. Explored space beyond
our blue-green bubble. But.

Hostages to 'what if?', we must be ready
for a future crater-making asteroid,
should one ever be discovered.
We craft a DART to deflate it, scan the skies
until we detect Didymos
with its swooping moonlet Dimorphos,
the perfect dancing pair to test our scheme.

We boldly launch our mission. Ten months later,
agog and goosebumped, scientists watch DART
crash as forecast into Dimorphos.
Mission-speak announces 'success threshold surpassed',
Dimorphos' curve is diverted, and we have proved
science fact protects us from science fiction.

(should one ever be discovered)

Time Machine

From opaque chaos, Big Bang fury gives way
to fundamental particles, formless clarity, the dawn of first light:

some repose for protons, bound with electrons in new-made atoms.
The first stars and galaxies coalesce in unmeasured time.

Light and matter travel far and farther, light waves lengthen
to cosmological red shift. Here and now,

JWST, telescopic time machine, uses coded stars
to calibrate itself. Sends its first images, its own first light.

Infrared illuminates stars and galaxies, forges a path backwards
to universal first light, to creation long ago, now far away.

The earth-bound CEERS team peers at red smudges, smears
of rare and precious photons: names galaxies for the next generation,

recalculates the numbers, so different from our first thoughts,
recalibrates the universe, and what we all may be.

The One Thing Brian Cox Taught Me

At the outer edges of our eyeballs,
184 million rod cells stand
ready for this low-light moment.

    We are seeing stars.

The tiny lights hover,
we are bathed in photon streams,
two lovers full of whispered dreams,

    starlight from faraway and forever

        star light
        star bright
        shine on my retina

              tonight.

A 13 billion light-year journey ends,
illuminates   us   with a flash
of rhodopsin   workaday magic.

    Ancient light is
        perceived,
            captured,
      persists,
            dances
              free in our eyes,

answering the lovers' eternal question…

so it is true, that nothing   in this moment
has existed   in quite this way before.

Tingsha

We wait on our mats, submitting.

Three bright notes shimmer, ring unhindered.
Signal us to the present.

Our bodies stretch imperceptibly upwards,
downwards as we reach more space inside ourselves.

The sweetness of the triple note sanctifies
the space, coils, binds us in sound

with an infinitesimal thread.
In the space between the notes is the music.

In the space between us is the music of our bodies:
re-tuned, returned to harmony.

The final three notes seal our effort, our journey,
the weightless notes that sustain us all.

Madonna of the Tube

She is transfigured by love,
besotted as she rocks and cossets

her precious one, astonishing newborn.
Her face is illuminated,

and with her much-practiced right hand
she manipulates the straps which keep

her child close to her body.
She taps and clucks wide-eyed to coax

a pseudo-smile from her tiny one,
its soft skull next to steel and grubby seats.

She even wears blue clothes.

A Midsummer Night's Dream

Unnoticed, I watch her. More iridescent than the rest,
she whirls and free-wheels in festival clothes that flutter
across continents: kaftan, kente, kimono,

braided and bowed like a present for me.
Those eyes, enormous from taking it all in.
She strokes her perfect cheek with a tiny hand,
and I burn for the graze of those fingertips.

Glamping this three-day party, she is here for the music,
the vibe, her daisied boots ready for mud. I am here
to serve her, keep her safe, my squawky-talkie
at the ready. Hi-viz. Access all areas.

My dreams are of keeping her beer cold,
hearing her laugh at my jokes. If she thinks I'm an ass,
well, the roofies will work like a charm.

Cold

Time wounds all heels – unknown

You break women in like shoes.

I know of three more after me.
You force your ego

into our perfect space,
claim we're the wrong shape:

not enough give, but better
once we know who's boss.

One had her shank-spirit broken;
still fragile, she skulks

in life's stock room, boxed
between misfits and odd sizes.

The others put on a bit of extra polish
then jumped back into the shop window,

their colour a little too loud, to mask
the shame and scuffs beneath.

Today, you don't notice me and my
killer heels as you strut wide-legged,

cock-happy in your latest size 12s.
I take your life, then steal your shoes,

leave you stilettoed.

Dainty

What good am I to you, legging it home late?
As much use as a chocolate teapot. Don't ask
why I'm glass, the words got twisted in translation.
As a metaphor it will do – bright, clear, pure:
just what you need to pounce a prince.
So here I am, tiny – oh yes, I have to be tiny –
my Chinese roots. No clodhoppers need apply.
And practical in my way:

when those stupid sisters lick their lips
desperate to fit, and chop their feet
to mutilated stumps, a quick spit and polish
then it's your turn.
He doesn't care you're in the ash,
at the bottom of the heap.
You're the right psychological profile.
Look under her skirts, princey, tucked away
is the other shoe. She is begging for it,
waiting to be rescued.

T for Temptation

Sinuous, Moga leans
backwards in abandon
at the syncopated feel
of deco jazz silk
on the backs of her legs.
She dances against the darkness
admired by the bright young
salarymen from Matsushita Electric.

Geisha flaunt their sex
with red silk in the cleft
of their split-peach hair: her bob
is hidden in a cloche bonnet.
But her tiny pink toe
works free from those red shoes,

shocks.

The salarymen look away, lifting their sake.
She dances against the darkness.

Pebble

They walk along the shore. Two sets of eyes
scan millions of years, thousands of pebbles.

Some with all their corners gone,
smoothed to offer no resistance.

Some holding secrets
only a shattering wave can reveal.

Some wet and shining for attention,
dulling as they dry.

Some with ridges, raised from mineral mendings
scarred, beautiful.

He hands her a pebble.
White quartz, quiet as an egg.

Her hand closes round it,
recognises its fit in her palm,

as it warms there.
Her pebble from the beach.

Cartographer

When your mother died, you said

each close death is seismic.

The tectonic plates of family
thrust youngest to middle,
daughter to matriarch,
the voice we thought gone

inhabits another.

We stare across the rift valley
resenting the lost.

Circle the mountain
of sibling rivalry.

Tame the bare rock
of perspective.

The old map,   obsolete as an ox-bow lake.

Molten, you burst into my life
blazing with heat to smelt my answering heart.

When you left, it was a tsunami
but I did not drown.

I made another map.

Notes

Cwen

Just one of the fourteen burial mounds at the Anglo-Saxon site of Sutton Hoo contained a female.

She was a high-status woman, perhaps a queen, and possibly the decision-maker responsible for creating the famous ship burial.

Smickling

Smickling was a folk belief in wearing the shoes of a woman who had recently given birth to help a childless woman conceive.

Pilgrim

This poem is in the shape of a shoe-shaped lead model brought to Rievaulx Abbey, possibly by a pilgrim, now on display there.

The World Turns

Smalti are small pieces of coloured glass mosaic (often Venetian), made in the same traditional way for hundreds of years.

AKA Janus

Charles W Leadbeater brought the concept of chakras to the West in 1927. He used Newtonian rainbow colours in his descriptions of them: the original Vedas and Upanishads had made no mention of colours.

Brave New World

The Radium Girls from Orange County New Jersey successfully took the Radium Dial Co. to court in a ground-breaking legal case after contracting radium poisoning from following instructions to 'point' their brushes on their lips.

Shoes on the Danube

The sculpture created in 2005 by Gyula Pauer commemorates those killed in Budapest by the fascist Arrow Cross militiamen in 1944-45.

Strike Hard, Strike Sure

The title is the motto of Bomber Command. East Kirkby Aviation Centre in Lincolnshire displays items recovered from the airfields after WW2 sorties and bombing raids.

Charm

From medieval times until the late 1800s shoes were concealed in the building fabric of many dwellings, it is thought to ward off evil spirits. The Northampton Museum and Art Gallery keeps an index of concealed shoes as they are found in UK homes.

A Midsummer Night's Dream

Roofies is a street name for the drug Rohypnol.

Time Machine

JWST: James Webb Space Telescope

CEERS: Cosmic Evolution Early Release Science, a cosmological survey using JWST observations.

Cold

The first line of this work appears in a poem in Rupi Kaur's collection *the sun and her flowers*.

T for Temptation

The image on which this poem is based is a Japanese woodcut by Kiyoshi Kobayakawa called 'The Dancer'. Moga was a term for a modern young woman during the Meiji era (1868-1912), a period that saw much industrial growth in Japan.

Acknowledgements

Versions of some of these poems have been previously published in: *Allegro, Consilience, Dust, Envoi, Dawn Treader, Dream Catcher, Ink Sweat and Tears, Pennine Platform, Raceme* and *South*.

Five Leaves New Poetry

Five Leaves presents a new series of debut poetry pamphlets by East Midlands writers, showcasing the exciting range of emerging talent from our region.

1. *She Will Allow Her Wings* **Jane Bluett**
   978-1-915434-09-8, 40 pages, £7, June 2023

2. *Beyond Caring* **Trish Kerrison**
   978-1-915434-10-4, 40 pages, £7, September 2023

3. *North by Northnorth* **Elvire Roberts**
   978-1-915434-12-8, 44 pages, £7, December 2023

4. *The Stories In Between* **Teresa Forrest**
   978-1-915434-11-1, 32 pages, £7, December 2023

5. *Keep All the Parts* **Roy Young**
   978-1-915434-13-5, 34 pages, £7, March 2024

6. *Relief Map* **Jan Norton**
   978-1-915434-14-2, 33 pages, £7, March 2024

7. *New Uses for a Wand* **Fiona Theokritoff**
   978-1-915434-16-6, 40 pages, £7, June 2024

8. *You Worry Too Much* **Nathan Fidler**
   978-1-915434-17-3, 32 pages, £7, June 2024

All pamphlets can be ordered from our websites.

Five Leaves Publications/Bookshop
14a Long Row, Nottingham NG1 2DH
0115 837 3097

info@fiveleaves.co.uk   bookshop@fiveleaves.co.uk
www.fiveleaves.co.uk   www.fiveleavesbookshop.co.uk